My First Pocket Guide

New Hampshire

By Carole Marsh

The GALLOPADE GANG

Carole Marsh
Bob Longmeyer
Chad Beard
Cecil Anderson
Steven Saint-Laurent
Jill Sanders
Kathy Zimmer
Terry Briggs
Pat Newman
Billie Walburn
Jackie Clayton
Pam Dufresne
Cranston Davenport
Lisa Stanley
Antoinette Miller
Victoria DeJoy
Al Fortunatti
Shery Kearney

Published by GALLOPADE INTERNATIONAL

www.newhampshireexperience.com

800-536-2GET • www.gallopade.com

Gallopade is proud to be a member of these educational organizations and associations:

Other New Hampshire Experience Products

- The New Hampshire Experience!
- The BIG New Hampshire Reproducible Activity Book
- The New Hampshire Coloring Book
- My First Book About New Hampshire!
- New Hampshire "Jography": A Fun Run Through Our State
- New Hampshire Jeopardy!: Answers and Questions About Our State
- The New Hampshire Experience! Sticker Pack
- The New Hampshire Experience! Poster/Map
- Discover New Hampshire CD-ROM
- New Hampshire "Geo" Bingo Game
- New Hampshire "Histo" Bingo Game

A Word From the Author... (okay, a few words)...

Hi!

Here's your own handy pocket guide about the great state of New Hampshire! It really will fit in a pocket–I tested it. And it really will be useful when you want to know a fact you forgot, to bone up for a test, or when your teacher says, "I wonder . . ." and you have the answer–instantly! Wow, I'm impressed!

Get smart, have fun!

Carole Marsh

New Hampshire Basics explores your state's symbols and their special meanings!

New Hampshire Geography digs up the what's where in your state!

New Hampshire History is like traveling through time to some of your state's great moments!

New Hampshire People introduces you to famous personalities and your next-door neighbors!

New Hampshire Places shows you where you might enjoy your next family vacation!

New Hampshire Nature - no preservatives here, just what Mother Nature gave to New Hampshire!

All the real fun stuff that we just HAD to save for its own section!

Who Named You?

New Hampshire's official state name is...

State Name

New Hampshire

OFFICIAL: appointed, authorized, or approved by a government or organization

Statehood: June 21, 1788

New Hampshire was the 9th state to join the Union.

New Hampshire's state-commemorative quarter was issued in 2000. Look for it in cash registers everywhere!

Coccinella noemnotata is my name (that's Latin for ladybug)! What's YOURS?

What's In A Name?

New Hampshire got its name from John Mason of the Plymouth Council, who was given a large tract of land in New England by King James I. John Mason named his new land New Hampshire for his home county of Hampshire in England.

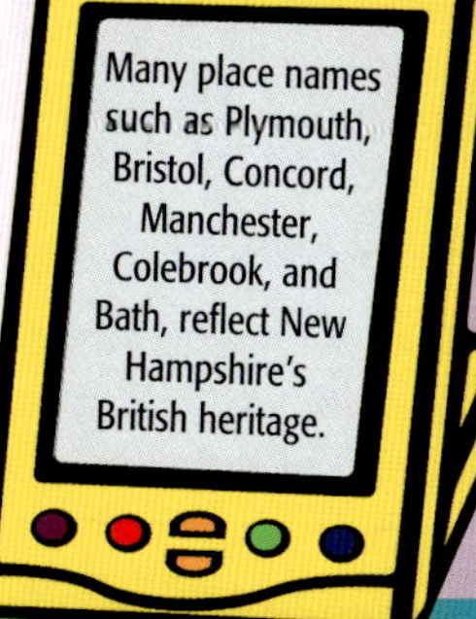

WHO Are You Calling Names?

State Nicknames

The Granite State

New Hampshire is not the only name by which the state is recognized. Like many other states, New Hampshire has some nicknames, official or unofficial!

State Capital: Concord

Became the capital in 1808

In 1819, the state legislature met for the first time in the new State House in Concord. The State House took five years to build. It's a magnificent building made with New Hampshire granite and trimmed with Vermont marble.

The New Hampshire State House is the nation's oldest state capitol where the legislature still meets in its original chambers.

Word Definition

CAPITAL: a town or city that is the official seat of government
CAPITOL: the building in which the government officials meet

Who's in Charge Here?

New Hampshire's GOVERNMENT has three branches:

LEGISLATIVE	EXECUTIVE	JUDICIAL
The legislative branch is called the General Court.		
Two Houses: The Senate (24 members) House of Representatives (400 members)	A governor, and an executive council	Supreme Court (five members) Superior Court

Home rule rules! Each spring, New Hampshire towns hold town meetings. All the town's voters are given a chance to be heard. All voters then vote directly on the issues, instead of delegating this privilege to an elected body of legislators.

With 424 members, the New Hampshire General Court is one of the largest, elected law-making bodies in the world!

State Flag

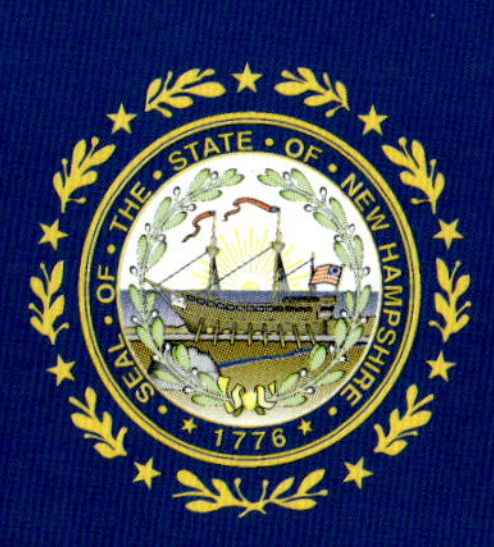

State Flag

New Hampshire's current state flag was adopted in 1909.

It features the state seal on a blue field surrounded by laurel leaves and nine stars showing New Hampshire was the ninth state to join the Union.

As you travel throughout New Hampshire, count the times you see the New Hampshire flag! Look for it on government vehicles, too!

State Seal

The state seal of New Hampshire features the frigate *Raleigh*, resting on stocks in Portsmouth, depicting the state's rich history of shipbuilding. The sun rises over the Atlantic Ocean. The date on the bottom of the seal is 1776. A wreath of laurel leaves encircles the seal.

Word Definition

MOTTO: a sentence, phrase, or word expressing the spirit or purpose of an organization or group

State Motto

New Hampshire's state motto is...

"Live Free or Die."

The state motto was taken from a quote by General John Stark, a distinguished hero of the Revolutionary War. The full quote is, "Live free or die; death is not the worst of evils."

The Legislature made "Live Free or Die" the official state motto in 1945.

Birds of a Feather

Purple Finch

—*Carpodacus purpureus*—

Purple finches live in pine trees during the summer and move to thickets and shrubs for the cold winter months. They feed on seeds, flower buds, and plant shoots.

The purple finch isn't purple at all! The scientific name means "purple fruit eater." The female is brown and the male is brownish with a red head and breast. The purple finch sings a long, beautiful warbling song. Its call is a *tik* or *tuk*.

The New Hampshire hen and the chickadee were also nominated, but the purple finch was voted into the office of New Hampshire's state bird.

White Birch

—*Betula papyrifera*—

So was I once myself a swinger of birches.
And so I dream of going back to be.
—Robert Frost

The beautiful white birch is native to New Hampshire and found in all regions of the state. It grows on richly wooded slopes and along lakes and streams. The bark is creamy white edged with yellow and peels in thin layers.

A lovelier flower on earth was never sown.
—William Wordsworth

The purple lilac isn't native to New Hampshire or North America. The lovely purple flower was brought from England in 1750 and planted at the home of Governor Benning Wentworth in Portsmouth. It was adopted as the state flower in 1919. Purple lilacs bloom beautifully throughout New Hampshire. Rochester is known as the Lilac City.

RIDDLE:

If the state wildflower got mixed up with the state bird, what would you have?

ANSWER: A purple bird that wears pink lady's slippers—it could happen!

White-tailed Deer

—Odocoileus virginianus—

State Animal

New Hampshire's state animal, the white-tailed deer, was important to Native Americans and early colonists. They used deer meat (venison) for food and the hide to make shoes, clothing, blankets, and even shelters.

White-tailed deer are so named because the underside of their tails are white.

The white-tailed deer was named the New Hampshire state animal in 1983.

RED SPOTTED NEWT

—Notophthalmus viridescens—

Students at Goffstown High School campaigned for two years to have the red spotted newt named the official state amphibian. In 1985, the students succeeded and the red spotted newt was designated state amphibian.

Red spotted newts are perfect ecological symbols because they live in areas greatly affected by acid rain. Newts live in small pools of water, so it's easier to see the effects of acid rain on their homes!

Less acid rain = more newts!

More acid rain = fewer newts!

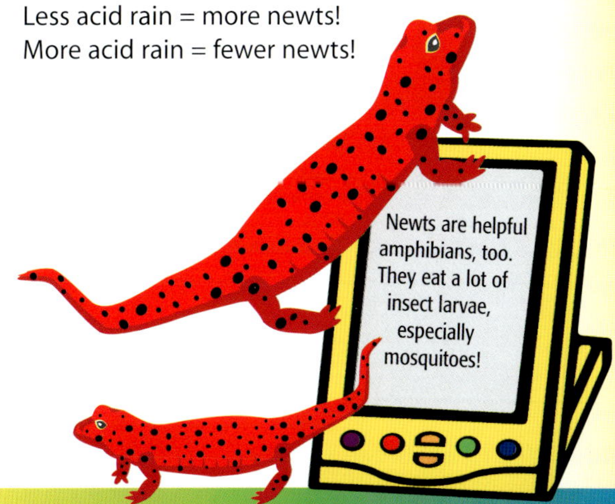

State Rock

Granite is "the rock" of New Hampshire. Although New Hampshire is called the Granite State, mining only contributes a small part to the state's economy. High-quality granite is still quarried in almost all of New Hampshire's counties.

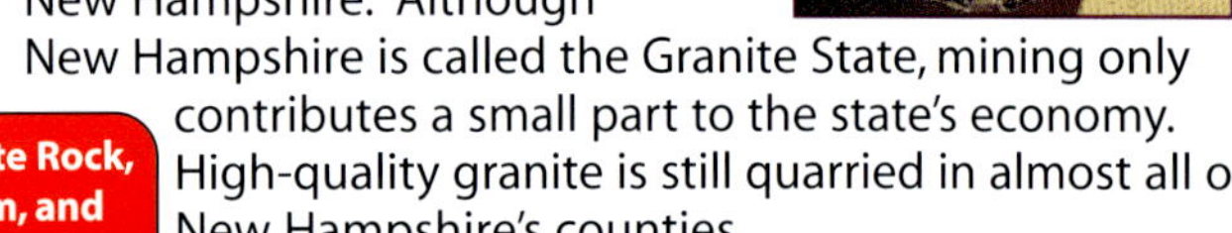

State Rock, Gem, and Mineral

Granite is formed when rock that's been melted by heat cools very slowly deep inside mountains. Granite is usually light gray or pink. It's a very hard stone and often used in highway and building construction.

State Gem

Smoky quartz is the state gem. It's found in many types of rocks, including granite. Quartz is the most common silicate, or glass mineral. One quartz crystal can weigh up to 70 tons (63 metric tons)! That's one BIG rock! Quartz is used in watches and clocks!

State Mineral

Beryl is a gemstone found in granite rocks. It's the state mineral of New Hampshire. Beryl crystals are yellow to yellow-green in color and can be up to 30 feet (9 meters) long! Emeralds and aquamarines are types of beryl and are used to make beautiful jewelry.

State Sport

Skiing became a popular sport in New Hampshire during the 1930s. In 1931, the Boston and Maine Railroad ran "snow trains" to carry skiers between Boston and North Conway. The Boston and Maine carried skiers to northern New Hampshire for many years.

Today, dozens of trails, lodges, and lifts provide many snowy opportunities for the skiing enthusiast. Loon Mountain, Waterville Valley, and Mount Washington's valleys are special spots for snow skiing.

New Hampshire adopted skiing as the official state sport in 1998.

New Hampshire has the nation's first snow ski club, first ski school, first cleared ski trail, and first overhead tow.

State Songs

New Hampshire has many state songs, one official and eight honorary:

Official State Song:

"**Old New Hampshire**" adopted in 1949
words by Dr. John F. Holmes
music by Maurice Hoffman

Honorary State Songs:

"**New Hampshire, My New Hampshire**"
words by Julius Richelson
music by Walter P. Smith

"**New Hampshire Hills**"
words by Paul Scott Maurer
music by Tom Powers

"**Autumn in New Hampshire**"
by Leo Austin

"**New Hampshire's Granite State**"
by Annie B. Currier

"**Oh, New Hampshire**"
by Brownie McIntosh

"**The Old Man of the Mountain**"
by Paul Belanger

"**The New Hampshire State March**"
by Rene Richards

"**New Hampshire Naturally**"
by Rick Shaw and Ron Shaw

State Insect

Ladybug Beetle

(Coccinella noemnotata)

Farmers welcome the bright orange-colored ladybugs because they dine on small pests which destroy plants and fruit trees.

On cold, frosty days, you might find a large swarm (group) of ladybugs huddled together under a piece of bark—that's where they go to hibernate for the winter.

State Butterfly

The tiny Karner blue (*Lycaeides melissa samuelis*) was designated New Hampshire's official state butterfly in 1992. The beautiful Karner blue, or Melissa blue, is an endangered species because it's losing its habitat or home.

Hey birdie, watch out! Ladybugs might look like a yummy snack–but, they actually taste pretty bad!

Hi! Remember me? I was designated New Hampshire's state insect in 1977!

Brook Trout

(Salvelinus fontinalis)

State Fish

The brook trout lives in lakes, ponds, and streams throughout the state. Trout are silvery-brown or rainbow-colored and prefer colder water—especially for spawning (having babies). It's a favored fish of finicky fishermen!

New Hampshire Trout

Put a brook trout filet on foil. Drizzle with lemon juice. Sprinkle with salt and pepper. Add shredded smoked ham and broil fish until done.

Sounds fishy to me!

The State of New Hampshire

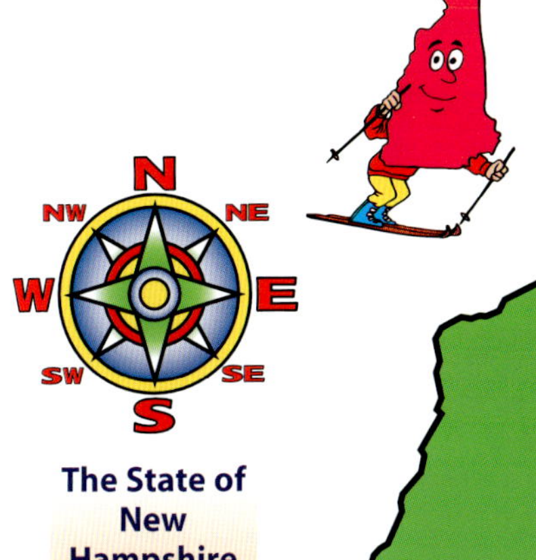

The State of New Hampshire is roughly shaped like a right triangle. It ranks 44th in total area among the 50 states.

States are great!

State Location

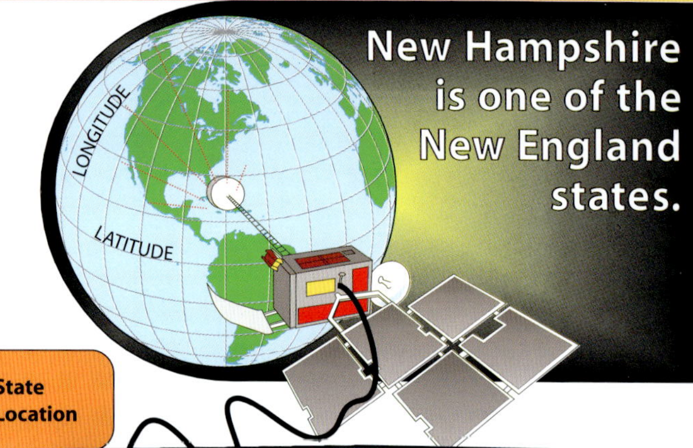

State Location

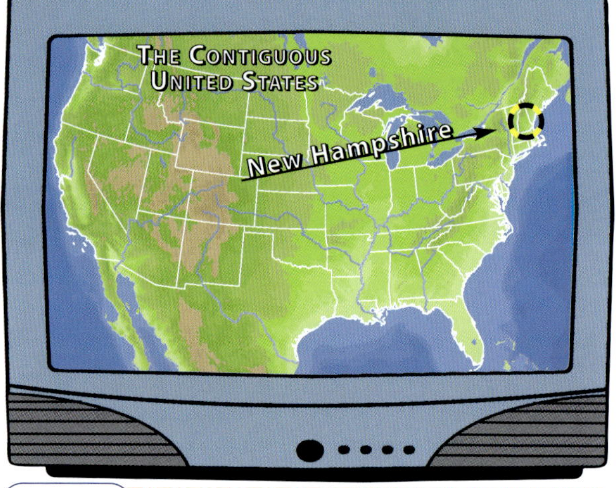

LATITUDE: Imaginary lines which run horizontally east and west around the globe

LONGITUDE: Imaginary lines which run vertically north and south around the globe

On The Border!

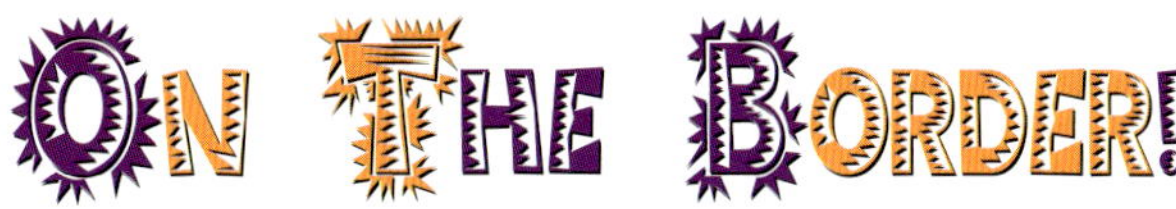

These border New Hampshire:

States: Maine, Vermont, Massachusetts

Country: Canada

Bodies of water: Atlantic Ocean
Connecticut River
Salmon Falls River
Piscataqua River

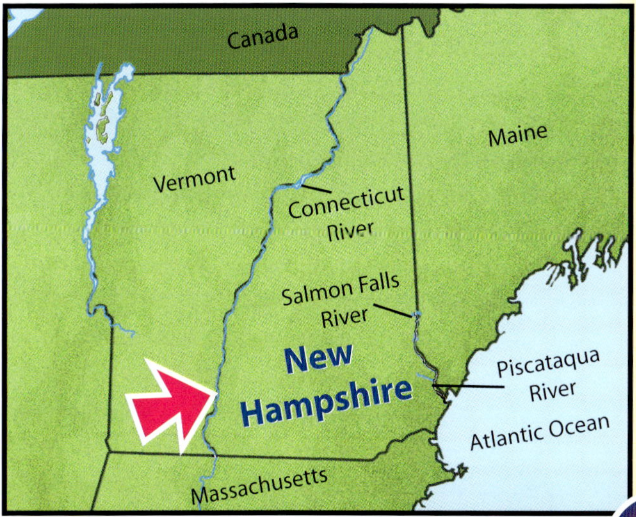

I'll Take the Low Road...

East-West, North-South, Area

New Hampshire is 93 miles (150 kilometers) from east to west—or west to east. Either way, it's not a very long drive!

Total Area: Approx. 9,283 square miles
(24,041 square kilometers)
Land Area: Approx. 8,969 square miles
(23,228 square kilometers)

New Hampshire stretches 190 miles (306 kilometers) from north to south—or south to north. Either way, it's *still* not a very long drive!

You Take the High Road!

Highest Point
Mount Washington—6,288 feet (1,917 meters)

Visitors find three ways to "climb" Mount Washington: on foot, by cog railway from Crawford Notch, and by auto on the road from Glen House that's open mid-May to mid-October.

Lowest Point
Sea level along the Atlantic Ocean

I'm County-ing on You!

New Hampshire is divided into 10 counties.

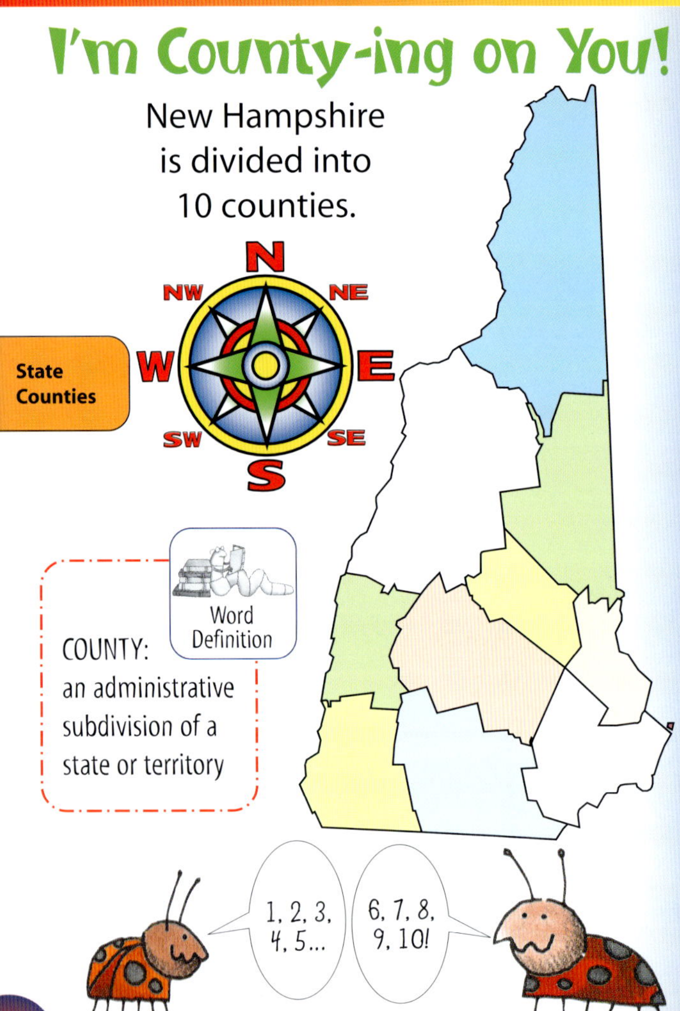

COUNTY: an administrative subdivision of a state or territory

It's All Natural!

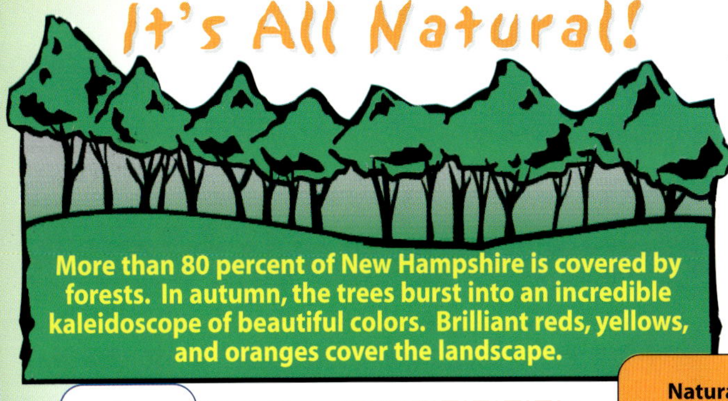

More than 80 percent of New Hampshire is covered by forests. In autumn, the trees burst into an incredible kaleidoscope of beautiful colors. Brilliant reds, yellows, and oranges cover the landscape.

Natural Resources

Word Definition

NATURAL RESOURCES: things that exist in or are formed by nature

Minerals and rocks:

Granite	Mica
Sand	Feldspar
Gravel	Beryl

Ruggles Mine in the White Mountains is the oldest and most spectacular mica, feldspar, beryl, and uranium mine in the nation! It's a great place for rock hounds to do some digging!

Weather, Or Not?!

New Hampshire's temperatures can drop to 9°F (-13°C) in the winter and reach 83°F (28°C) in the summer.

Highest temperature: 106°F (41°C), Nashua, July 4, 1911

°F=Degrees Fahrenheit °C=Degrees Celsius

Lowest temperature: -46°F (-43°C), Pittsburg, January 28, 1925

New Hampshire's summers are relatively short and cool. The winters are long and severe with heavy snows in the mountains.

Back On Top

New Hampshire's topography includes mountains, valleys, lakes, rivers, falls, forests, islands, and shores. New Hampshire has three land regions; the **Coastal Lowlands**, the **New England Upland**, and the **White Mountains**.

TOPOGRAPHY: the detailed mapping of the features of a small area or district

Glaciers moved across the rocky land millions of years ago shaping New Hampshire's mountains and carving valleys and lake beds.

King of the Hill

Mountains

- Mount Washington
- Mount Chocorua
- Mount Monadnock
- Mount Sunapee

Ranges

Mountains and Ranges

In and around the White Mountains, there are 48 peaks that top 4,000 feet (1,219 meters). When a hiker climbs all 48 mountains, he or she can become a member of the Four Thousand Footer Club—an official "peak bagger."

- White Mountains
- Franconia Range
- Sandwich Range
- Kinsman Range
- Kilkenny Range
- Carter-Moriah Range
- Presidential Range
- Western Highlands

Franconia, Kinsman, and Crawford are some of New Hampshire's neat notches!

A River Runs Through It!

Here are some of New Hampshire's major rivers:

- **Connecticut River**
- **Merrimack River**
- **Pemigewasset River**
- **Winnipesaukee River**
- **Salmon Falls River**
- **Piscataqua River**
- **Androscoggin River**
- **Saco River**

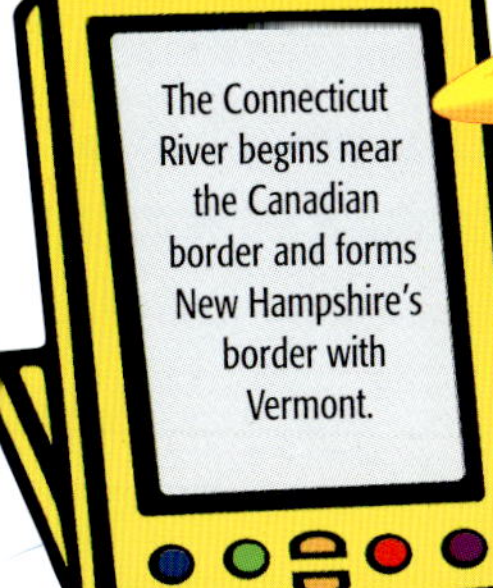

Gone Fishin'

Some of New Hampshire's lakes:

- Lake Winnipesaukee
- First Connecticut Lake
- Second Lake
- Lake Francis
- Newfound Lake
- Moore Reservoir
- Back Lake
- Conway Lake
- Stinson Lake
- Squam Lake
- Ossipee Lake
- Lake Sunapee
- Blackwater Reservoir
- Umbagog Lake

RESERVOIR: a body of water stored for public use

ARE YOU A CITY MOUSE... OR A COUNTRY MOUSE?

Have you heard of these wonderful New Hampshire town, city, or crossroad names? Perhaps you can start your own list!

LARGER CITIES:
- Concord
- Portsmouth
- Manchester
- Nashua
- Rochester
- Dover
- Keene
- Claremont
- Derry
- Laconia
- Londonderry
- Merrimack

UNIQUE NAMES:
- Unity
- Center Sandwich
- Rumney
- Orange
- Intervale
- Rindge
- Dublin
- Jaffrey
- West Swanzey
- Spofford
- Ossipee
- Goffstown

Major Highways

I-89
I-93
I-95
F.E. Everett Turnpike
Spaulding Turnpike

Railroads

New Hampshire has about 355 miles (571 kilometers) of railroad track currently in use. Scenic trains include Winnipesaukee Scenic Railroads, Conway Scenic Railway, and the famous Mount Washington Cog Railway.

Major Airports

New Hampshire's main airport is in Manchester. There are more than 50 airports and heliports throughout the state.

Seaports

Portsmouth is an important port and has been since colonial times. The deep-water port is ice-free all year. More than 250,000 tons (226,796 metric tons) of cargo are shipped through Portsmouth each year.

Timeline

1614	English Captain John Smith arrives
1622	John Mason receives grant of land from Britain's King James I; later names land New Hampshire
1623	David Thomson establishes first European settlement
1641	New Hampshire settlements put themselves under Massachusetts' jurisdiction
1679–80	New Hampshire becomes separate royal colony
1685	New Hampshire and other colonies form Dominion of New England
1689–97	French and Indian Wars are fought
1774	Paul Revere takes his midnight ride announcing buildup of British military forces in Massachusetts
1775	Revolutionary War begins
1776	New Hampshire adopts temporary constitution; signs national Declaration of Independence
1788	New Hampshire becomes ninth state of the Union
1861–65	Civil War is fought; 39,000 New Hampshire troops fight for the Union
1929	First U.S. ski school is established at Sugar Hill
1966	Home rule is granted to New Hampshire cities
1990	Despite protests from New Hampshire environmentalists, Seabrook Nuclear Plant begins operation

On to the 21st Century!

Here come the humans!

Thousands of years ago, ancient peoples inhabited present-day New Hampshire. They may have originally come across a frozen bridge of land between Asia and Alaska. If so, they slowly traveled east until some settled in what would one day become the state of New Hampshire.

Ancient artifacts and yabba-dabba doo-dads have been found at Lake Winnipesaukee. Some of these historical relics appear to be more than 9,000 years old!

These early people were nomadic hunters who traveled in small bands. They camped when seasons offered hunting, fishing, and fruit and nut gathering.

Native Americans Once Ruled!

By AD 1500, the Pennacook, descendants of the first ancient people, lived in the woodlands of New Hampshire. The Abnaki and Pennacook were Algonquin tribes of hunters, fishermen, and farmers. Families lived in dome-shaped wigwams made by the Native American women out of tree bark and animal skins.

When European explorers arrived in New Hampshire in the early 17th century, there were probably about 5,000 Native Americans living there.

Word Definition

WAMPUM: beads, pierced and strung, used by Indians as money or for ornaments

Land Ho!

The first explorers to visit New Hampshire may have been Viking sailors from Norway as far back as the 11th century. Or perhaps the first visitors were Europeans who fished New Hampshire's waters in the 1400s.

The first recorded visits were made in the 1600s by English and French explorers looking for new lands and natural resources such as fish and beaver pelts.

King James I of Great Britain received reports from British explorers of the New World's lush forests and abundant wildlife. The king claimed the land, and his son, Prince Charles, named it New England.

King James I

Home, Sweet Home

In 1620, the Council for New England was formed in Great Britain. Through a charter from the king, the council had authority to issue land grants in the New World.

One large grant, part of present-day New Hampshire and Maine, was given to John Mason and Sir Ferdinando Gorges in 1622. Mason named his portion New Hampshire and sent settlers across the sea to establish colonies.

By 1641, four New Hampshire towns had been established—Portsmouth, Exeter, Dover, and Hampton. The towns were too small to stand alone, so they became part of the Massachusetts Bay Colony. In 1679, the king of England made New Hampshire a separate royal colony.

The first European settlement in New Hampshire was founded in 1623 by Scotsman David Thomson. He established Pannaway Plantation at the site of present-day Rye, a settlement that lasted only a few years.

Early New Hampshirites

Good fences make good neighbors.
—Robert Frost

New Hampshire's settlers came to a New World full of promise and opportunity, but there were many challenges, too! Early settlers had to clear the land of trees and large rocks. Lumber from the trees was used to build homes and furniture. Settlers moved the rocks to clear the land for farming and placed them together to form low stone walls around their land. The stone walls are still in place today and have become a symbol of colonial New Hampshire.

BIG FOOT Was *Here?*

In 1977, a dealer and two young helpers were startled one night by a BIG 8-foot (2.4-meter) furry creature while they were setting up for a Hollis flea market. The creature left BIG footprints more than 16 inches (41 centimeters) long. *Was it BIG FOOT?* The dealer and his helpers didn't wait to find out! Two other dealers reported their truck being shaken by BIG furry hands. They didn't wait around either, but tracks found by their truck matched the other BIG footprints!

Other BIG, hairy sightings have occurred around Sandwich, at Mount Israel, and at Sandwich Dome. These sightings have even been "recorded" by 3-foot (1-meter) footprints—with four toes and no claws—that were found in mud near the sightings. Everyone who saw him said BIG FOOT seemed just as frightened as they were and ran off into the woods!

French and Indian Wars

For the first 50 years, European settlers and Native Americans lived together peacefully in New Hampshire. As more settlers moved in, tensions increased. Settlers' livestock often ruined Native Americans' fields. Settlers and Native Americans argued about rights to hunting and fishing grounds.

Tensions turned into arguments! Arguments turned into wars! From 1689 to 1760, New Hampshire was a battleground between France and England as the two countries struggled to control North America. New Hampshire's Algonquin tribes sided with the French to fight against the English settlers and their comrades, the Iroquois.

French and Indian Wars

In New Hampshire, the bloodiest battles occurred during King William's War (1689–1697) and Queen Anne's War (1702–1713). Almost 300 settlers were killed. Settlers retaliated by burning crops and villages. By 1730, most of the surviving Native Americans left New Hampshire.

Freedom! Freedom!

Some colonists felt England ignored their ideas and concerns. The French and Indian Wars had been very costly, so England tried to raise money by imposing taxes. Colonists objected to paying taxes to a motherland that was no longer their home.

In 1775, the colonies went to war with England. After the battles of Lexington and Concord, Massachusetts, hundreds of New Hampshire's Minutemen left home to help the colonists fight the British forces. Portsmouth became an important port for colonial privateers attacking British warships.

In January 1776, New Hampshire adopted its own constitution and became the first state to form a government separate from Great Britain. On July 4, 1776, the Declaration of Independence was signed. In 1781, New Hampshire's troops fought bravely in the Battle of Yorktown—the battle that won the war! Peace was finally declared in 1783. In 1789, George Washington was inaugurated as the first president of the United States of America!

Brother

The Civil War (1861–1865) was fought over slavery and the right of states to make their own individual decisions. The Confederacy, or Southern states, with plantations and slaves, were on one side of the conflict. The Union, or Northern states opposed slavery or had no need for it, and were on the other side. Some states remained neutral.

The Civil War

No Civil War battles were fought in New Hampshire, but New Hampshirites strongly supported the Union. As many as 39,000 men, almost half the state's male population, joined the Union forces. The first enlisted Union soldier to lose his life in the fighting was Luther C. Ladd from Alexandria.

On April 9, 1865, the Confederacy surrendered at Appomattox Court House in Virginia. It took years for the country to recover from the devastation of this unfortunate war, in which Americans could find no way to agree, except to fight.

Word Definition

RECONSTRUCTION: the recovery and rebuilding period following the Civil War

Brother vs. Brother

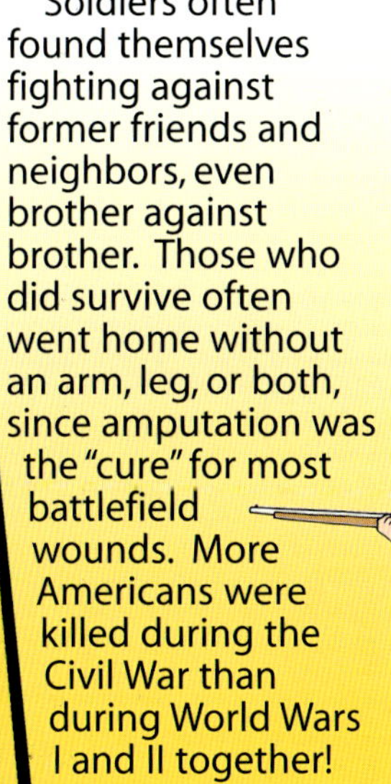

Soldiers often found themselves fighting against former friends and neighbors, even brother against brother. Those who did survive often went home without an arm, leg, or both, since amputation was the "cure" for most battlefield wounds. More Americans were killed during the Civil War than during World Wars I and II together!

In 1863, President Abraham Lincoln's Emancipation Proclamation, freed slaves still under Confederate control. In 1865, the 13th Amendment abolished slavery in the U.S.

Get It In Writing!

1756
State's first newspaper, *New Hampshire Gazette*, is published in Portsmouth

January, 1776
New Hampshire's first state constitution

July, 1776
Declaration of Independence

1784
Present state constitution is adopted

1788
New Hampshire is ninth and deciding vote to ratify U.S. Constitution

1905
Treaty ending Russo-Japanese War is signed at Portsmouth

Welcome To America!

People have come to New Hampshire from other states and other countries on almost every continent! As time goes by, New Hampshire's population grows more diverse. This means that people of different races and from different cultures and ethnic backgrounds have moved to New Hampshire. All New Hampshirites benefit from this diverse culture!

In the past, many immigrants have come to New Hampshire from England, France, Ireland, Scotland, Holland, Germany, Canada, and Iceland. More recently, people have migrated to New Hampshire from Hispanic countries such as Mexico, Asia, and the Pacific Islands. The state is proud of its heritage, including Native-Americans and African-Americans.

Only a certain number of immigrants are allowed to move to America each year. Many of these immigrants eventually become U.S. citizens.

HEY BROTHER, CAN YOU SPARE A DIME?

During the Great Depression of the 1930s, factories in New Hampshire close and wages decrease.

WATER'S RISING!

In 1936, spring floods ravage New Hampshire and cause more than $8 million in property damage.

BRRRRRR!

In 1978, a blizzard blows through and causes extensive damage through the state.

SHOO!

In 1981, swarms of gypsy moths cause massive defoliation.

NEW HAMPSHIRE STARTS HERE AND ENDS THERE!

In 1740, New Hampshire's eastern and southern boundaries are set by a royal commission which settles the dispute between New Hampshire and Massachusetts.

In 1764, New Hampshire's western boundary is set at the western bank of the Connecticut River which settles the dispute with New York.

QUITTING TIME!

In 1847, the state legislature enacts a 10-hour workday law for factory workers.

VOTE!

In 1909, New Hampshire adopts a direct primary law.

TIMBER!

The 1981 Forest Resources Planning Act regulates how New Hampshire's forests can be used.

DON'T BE LATE FOR SCHOOL!

In 1647, New Hampshire passes an act requiring towns of 50 families to establish schools to teach reading and writing. Towns of 100 families or more must establish a grammar school.

STRIKE!

On December 30, 1828, about 400 female mill workers walk out of the Dover Cotton Factory. This is the first women's strike in the U.S. The Dover mill girls have to give in and go back to work when the mill owners begin advertising for replacement employees.

YOU CAN'T MISS SCHOOL!

In 1871, the state legislature passes a law making school attendance mandatory!!

SUFFRAGE!

In 1920, the 19th Amendment gives women in the U.S. the right to vote!

Fight! Fight! Fight!

Wars that had an impact on New Hampshire:

- French and Indian Wars
- Revolutionary War
- War of 1812
- Mexican-American War
- Civil War
- Spanish-American War
- World War I
- World War II
- Korean War
- Vietnam War
- Persian Gulf War

Old Man of the Mountain

Way up on the top of Profile Mountain lives a man—a very special man! He's the "Old Man of the Mountain," a remarkable granite rock formation which looks like the profile of a man's face.

The "Old Man of the Mountain" is one of the most-famous natural landmarks in New Hampshire. His head measures 40 feet (12 meters) from chin to forehead. The "Old Man" lives 1,200 feet (366 meters) above Echo Lake.

The "Old Man" has inspired countless authors and artists. He has become the symbol of the people of New Hampshire—resolute, steadfast, loyal, and independent!

Indian Tribes

Pennacook Tribes

- Amoskeag
- Nashua
- Piscataqua
- Souhegan
- Squamscot

Abnaki Tribes

- Ossipee
- Pequawket

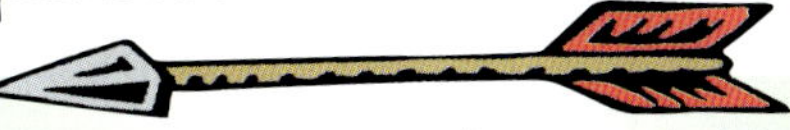

Native American men hunted deer, moose, beavers, and birds, and went ice fishing for trout. The women grew pumpkins, squash, beans, and *maize* (corn), and gathered berries and nuts from the forests. They tapped sap from sugar maple trees to make maple sugar and syrup.

European colonists exposed the Native Americans to deadly new diseases, such as smallpox and measles, to which they had no immunity. Thousands of Native Americans died.

Here, There, Everywhere!

Martin Pring—English explorer; sailed up the Piscataqua River in 1603; first European known to have explored present-day New Hampshire

Samuel de Champlain—French explorer; visited New Hampshire in 1605; mapped coasts of New Hampshire, Maine, and Massachusetts; took reports back to Europe of islands and a mainland rich in forests and abundant in wildlife

John Smith—English explorer; landed in 1614 on the Isles of Shoals and named them Smith's Islands; wrote a book entitled *A Description of New England* that guided the pilgrims to the colony of Massachusetts

Stephen Harriman Long—born in Hopkinton; explorer, naturalist, Army officer; led expeditions to Mississippi River and Rocky Mountains; Long's Peak in Colorado named in his honor

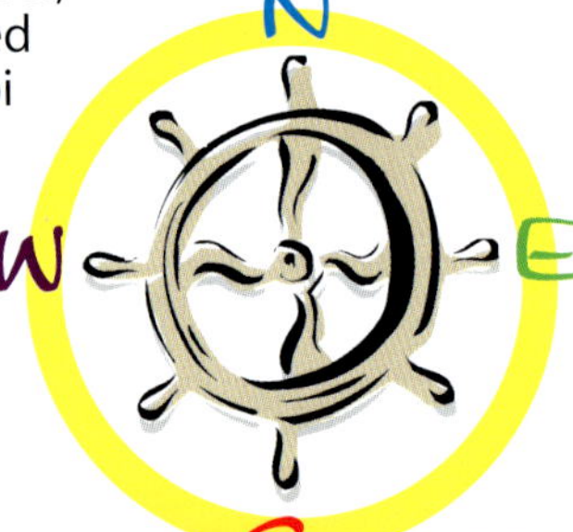

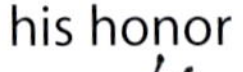

Founding Fathers

David Thomson—Scottish colonist; received land grant; sailed from Plymouth, England, with a small group of colonists; established Pannaway Plantation at the site of present-day Rye; settlement lasted only a few years

Edward and **William Hilton**—English brothers; established Hilton's Point, now the town of Dover

John Mason—English merchant; known as the Founder of New Hampshire; given large land grant by King James I; sent colonists to settle new land; named colony New Hampshire for Hampshire County, his home in England

John Wheelwright—clergyman from Massachusetts Bay Colony; established town of Exeter

Stephen Bachiler—clergyman from Massachusetts Bay Colony; founded town of Hampton

Founding Mothers

Mary Baker Eddy—born in Bow; religious leader; founded Christian Science which teaches healing of sickness through spiritual means; founded *Christian Science Monitor* daily newspaper

Laura Dewey Bridgman—born in Hanover; first American deaf and blind person to be successfully educated; attended Perkins Institution for the Blind in Boston

Authors

- **Robert Frost**—poet; Pulitzer Prize winner; wrote many poems about New England including collection of poems entitled *New Hampshire*

- **Eleanor Porter**—author; wrote many short stories; wrote novels including *Pollyanna* and *Pollyanna Grows Up*

- **Celia Thaxter**—poet; works include collection entitled *Driftwood*

- **Horace Greeley**—newspaper editor, political and social reformer, abolitionist; founded *New York Tribune*

- **Sarah Josepha Hale**—author, poet, editor, educator; editor of *Godey's Lady's Book,* wrote "Mary Had a Little Lamb"; founded Seaman's Aid Society; supported the building of the Bunker Hill Monument

- **William Loeb**—journalist, publisher of Manchester's *Union Leader* and *New Hampshire Sunday News*

- **John Irving**—author; wrote *The World According to Garp, The Hotel New Hampshire,* and *The Cider House Rules;* many of his works are set in New Hampshire

- **Grace de Repentigny Metalious**—author; wrote *Peyton Place*

Authors

- **Carroll Burleigh Colby**—author, artist; wrote children's stories about nature and adventure; wrote *Gobbit, the Magic Rabbit*

- **Edward Payson Dutton**—publisher; founded E.P. Dutton & Company publishing house

- **Charles Francis Hall**—author, explorer; led Arctic expeditions; wrote *Arctic Researches,* and *Life among the Esquimaux*

- **Alice Brown**—author; wrote children's books including *The Tiverton Tales* and *The Willoughbys*

- **J.D. Salinger**—author; wrote short stories; wrote novels, including *Catcher in the Rye*

- **Gladys Hasty Carroll**—author; wrote *As the Earth Turns*

- **Helen Dore Boylston**—author, nurse; used experiences in nursing as the background for her *Sue Barton* series of children's books

- **Thomas Bailey Aldrich**—author; editor of *Atlantic Monthly;* wrote "Story of a Bad Boy"

- **Tomie de Paola**—author, illustrator of *Strega Nona*; winner of Newbery and Caldecott awards

Do you know?

Which New Hampshire author wrote about a little lamb whose fleece was white as snow?

Answer: Sarah Josepha Hale in *Mary Had a Little Lamb*

DID SOMEONE SAY BOO!?

The town of Henniker is the home of "Ocean-Born Mary." She was born at sea in 1710. Shortly after her birth, pirates attacked the ship. The pirate leader promised not to harm the ship if the mother would name the child Mary after his own mother. The pirate even left a bolt of silk for her wedding dress.

Mary lived a long life. Since her death, residents report seeing a black carriage drive up to the house at night. The carriage stops, and a veiled figure descends and floats to a well where it drops a parcel before leaving in its ghostly coach. *What do you think might be in the package?* Mary's grave in the Quaker Cemetery is marked by a tombstone engraved "Widow Mary Wallace."

DO YOU BELIEVE IN GHOSTS?

Sports Stuff

Jenny Thompson—swimmer; today's most decorated U.S. Olympic female athlete; 2000 Women's Sports Foundation Sportswoman of the Year

Barbara Ann Cochran—skier; Olympic gold medal winner

Mike Flanagan—professional baseball player; pitcher for Baltimore Orioles and Toronto Blue Jays; won American League Cy Young Award

Red Rolfe—professional baseball player; infielder for New York Yankees; held American League records in hits and runs

Jane Blalock—professional golfer; won more than 30 professional tours

Carlton Fisk—professional baseball player; known as "The Catcher who Changed His Sox" after switching from Boston Red Sox to Chicago White Sox; held record for home runs by a catcher

The first college rowing contest was between boats and crews from Harvard and Yale. The race was held in 1853 on Lake Winnipesaukee.

Performing Artists

Amy Marcy Beach—pianist, composer; performed with Boston Symphony Orchestra; wrote *Gaelic Symphony,* first published symphonic work by a U.S. woman

Tom Rush—songwriter, blues singer; albums include *Late Night Radio*

Jonas Chickering—piano maker; built first grand piano with full iron frame in a single casing

Benjamin F. Keith—theatrical manager, entertainer; established vaudeville in the 1800s as a family type of entertainment; ran 400 vaudeville theaters across the country

James Broderick—actor; appeared in stage, movie, and TV productions; best-known as the father on the TV show *Family*

Henry Wilson Savage—theatrical producer; founded Boston Light Opera Company which performed opera in English and made ticket prices affordable

Circus owner P.T. Barnum called the view from the top of Mount Washington "the second greatest show on earth." His circus was known as "The Greatest Show on Earth."

Mandy Moore—singer, spokesperson; first album went platinum in just three months

Artists

Maxfield Parrish—illustrator, muralist; illustrated hundreds of magazines and books including *Mother Goose in Prose* and *The Arabian Nights*

Elizabeth Gardner Bouguereau—painter; first woman to have a painting exhibited at the Paris Salon of the French Academy of Art; first U.S. woman to receive a gold medal by the French Academy

Augustus Saint-Gaudens—sculptor; lived in Cornish where he founded an artists' colony; his lifelike sculptures include a statue of Abraham Lincoln in Chicago's Lincoln Park and the *Shaw Memorial* in Boston

Bob Montana—cartoonist; created the comic strip *Archie* that described the lives of American teenagers; based many characters on high school classmates in Manchester

Daniel French—sculptor; famous for statues honoring American heroes including *The Minute Man of Concord* and the seated statue of Abraham Lincoln in the Lincoln Memorial in Washington, D.C.

The beauty and charm of New Hampshire has inspired many noted artists and authors. The MacDowell Colony in Peterborough is an art colony in which talented artists are accepted as "fellows" and given a place to work.

Passaconaway—Pennacook leader; urged his people to keep peace with the European settlers; died from a disease brought by settlers

Mildred Custin—business executive; president of Bonwit Teller; first woman to head a major chain of retail stores

Eleazar Wheelock—educator, clergyman; founded Dartmouth College; first president of Dartmouth

Charles Augustus Young—astronomer; proved existence of chromosphere; determined sun's rate of rotation

John Henry Sununu—engineer, industrialist, politician, governor; chief of staff under President George Bush

Earl Tupper—inventor; creator of Tupperware; sales to stores were slow at first, but took off when Tupperware products were sold at home parties

Thaddeus S.C. Lowe—inventor, scientist, aeronaut; led balloon force during Civil War

John Wentworth—public official, royal governor; left New Hampshire at outbreak of Revolutionary War

Joseph Emerson Worcester—lexicographer; his dictionary went head to head with Noah Webster's dictionary, resulting in the "War of the Dictionaries"

Nicholas John Nicholas, Jr.—president and chief operating officer of Time, Inc.

More Very Important People

Sarah Ellen Palmer—physician; Fellow of American College of Surgeons

Kancamagus—last chief of the Pennacook in New Hampshire; led his people to Canada to escape the British attacks; highway that follows route to Canada is named in his honor

George Hoyt Whipple—pathologist; Nobel Prize winner for research in treating fatal blood disorder

Ralph Damon—airline executive; helped produce famous aircraft; president of American Airlines; president of Trans World Airlines

Stuart Chase—economist, author; advisor to President Franklin D. Roosevelt; coined phrase "The New Deal"

Zachariah Chandler—political activist; U.S. secretary of the interior; helped found Republican party

More Very Important People

Charles Alfred Pillsbury—industrialist; turned small flour company into world's largest flour producer

Ralph Cram—architect, author; designed Cathedral of St. John the Divine in New York City

Harlan Fiske Stone—educator, lawyer, jurist, U.S. attorney general, associate and chief U.S. Supreme Court justice

Meschech Weare—jurist; served as chief justice and first president (governor) of New Hampshire during Revolutionary War

Political Leaders

Franklin Pierce—14th president of the U.S., U.S. representative, U.S. senator; son of Benjamin Pierce

Daniel Webster—brilliant orator, lawyer, statesman, U.S. representative, U.S. secretary of state; first man elected to U.S. Senate Hall of Fame

Jeanne Shaheen—first elected woman governor of New Hampshire

Josiah Barlett—physician, statesman, politician; signer of Declaration of Independence; jurist and governor

Salmon Portland Chase—statesman, lawyer, jurist; U.S. secretary of state; created basis for present national banking system; U.S. Supreme Court chief justice; portrait is on the U.S. $10,000 bill

Elizabeth Gurley Flynn—political leader, social reformer; fought for better working conditions in factories throughout U.S.

Benning Wentworth—royal governor; helped New Hampshire separate from Massachusetts

Henry Wilson—teacher, businessman, abolitionist, U.S. vice president; helped found Free-Soil party

Henry Dearborn—Revolutionary War captain; U.S. secretary of war; major general in War of 1812

Alan Shepard, Jr.—first U.S. astronaut in space; commanded *Apollo 14* for third moon landing; fifth astronaut to walk on the moon

Christa McAuliffe—educator, astronaut; Concord high school teacher chosen by NASA to become first private citizen to go into space aboard the space shuttle *Challenger;* space shuttle exploded, all seven crew members died

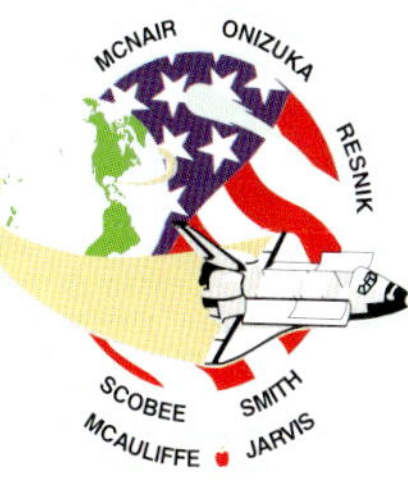

Robert Rogers—military officer; leader of Rogers' Rangers during French and Indian Wars

John Stark—military officer, served with Rogers' Rangers; American Revolutionary War general; statue of Stark represents New Hampshire in U.S. Capitol in Washington, D.C.

John Sullivan—soldier, politician; led one of first Revolutionary War attacks by colonists against the British; delegate to Continental Congress; governor; led state effort to ratify U.S. Constitution

William Whipple—Revolutionary War general; delegate to the Continental Congress; signer of Declaration of Independence

John Langdon—merchant; Continental Congress and Constitutional Convention delegate; signer of U.S. Constitution; governor and U.S. senator

Keeping the Faith

CHURCHES

St. John's Church, Portsmouth
First Congregational Society Unitarian Church, Hampton Falls
Grace Episcopal Church, Manchester
First Church, Nashua
First Church of Christ, Scientist, Concord
Society of Friends Meeting House, Dover
Congregational Church, Stoddard
Universalist Church, Alstead
United Church of Acworth
St. Mary's Catholic Church, Claremont
Orthodox Church of the Holy Resurrection, Berlin
Congregational Church of Christ, Berlin

SCHOOLS

Dartmouth College, Hanover
Franklin Pierce College, Rindge
New England College, Henniker
New Hampshire College, Manchester
Notre Dame College, Manchester
St. Anselm College, Manchester
Colby-Sawyer College, New London
University of New Hampshire, Durham
Phillips Exeter Academy, Exeter

HISTORIC SITES

Robert Frost Farm, Derry—"Stopping by the Woods on A Snowy Evening" is set in the Derry countryside

Greenfield Town Meeting House—oldest original meeting house in New Hampshire

Orford Street Historic District—includes The Ridge with seven historic homes

Saint-Gaudens National Historic Site, Cornish—home, studio, and workshop of the great sculptor

Shaker Village, Canterbury—settlement founded in 1792; more than 20 original buildings have been preserved

Strawbery Banke, Portsmouth—restored maritime village

PARKS

Franconia Notch State Park, White Mountains—home of the "Old Man of the Mountain"

White Mountain National Forest, northern New Hampshire

Mount Sunapee State Park, the Connecticut Valley

Odiorne State Park, marks spot where first European settlers landed in 1623

Historical Homes

Franklin Pierce Homestead Historic Site, Hillsboro—boyhood home of the 14th U.S. president

Pierce Manse, Concord—home where Franklin Pierce lived from 1842 to 1848; restored with many Pierce family furnishings

Daniel Webster Birthplace, Franklin

MacPheadris-Warner House, Portsmouth—oldest brick residence in the city

Castle in the Clouds, Moultonborough—home of Thomas G. Plant

John Paul Jones House, Portsmouth

Wentworth-Coolidge Mansion, Portsmouth—home of Benning Wentworth, New Hampshire's first royal governor

Richard Jackson House, Portsmouth—state's oldest home surviving in its original form

Governor John Langdon House, Portsmouth—now a property of the Society for the Preservation of New England Antiquities

Birthplace of Horace Greeley, Amherst

Mount Washington Hotel, Carroll—has hosted presidents, royalty, and celebrities

Birthplace of Salmon Portland Chase, Cornish—home of famous politician and jurist

A few of New Hampshire's famous Forts

- Fort Constitution in New Castle was the site of the first overt military action by the colonists during the Revolutionary War. Portsmouth colonials stormed the British fort and carried off arms and ammunition.

- Old Fort Number 4 in Charlestown is an authentic reproduction of a fortified village built by settlers in 1744 during the bloody French and Indian Wars.

Fort Constitution, first called Fort William and Mary, was the site of *two* raids by colonists, the first led by Major John Langdon following Paul Revere's news of British troops preparing to attack! Major John Sullivan led the second attack the very next day!

Libraries

Check out the following special New Hampshire libraries! (Do you have a library card? Have you worn it out yet?!)

Dartmouth College's Baker Memorial Library, Hanover

New Hampshire State Library, Concord

New Hampshire Historical Society Library, Concord

Ezekiel W. Dimond Library, University of New Hampshire in Durham

New Hampshire State Archives, Concord

The state's first free, tax-supported, public library was founded at Peterborough in 1833. Historians believe this to be the first free public library in the U.S.

Great Sights to See

- **Mystery Hill**, North Salem—America's Stonehenge; puzzling collection of stone walls, passageways, chambers, and carvings
- **Christa McAuliffe Planetarium**, Concord
- **Belknap-Sulloway Mill**, Laconia—oldest unaltered brick textile mill in the U.S.
- **Hebron Marsh Wildlife Sanctuary**, East Hebron
- **Isles of Shoals**—whale-watching and fishing
- **Fuller Gardens**, North Hampton—All America Rose Display Garden
- **Science and Nature Center**, Seabrook Station
- **Great Bay Estuarine Research Reserve**, near Newmarket—tidal waters, mud flats, salt marsh, and woodlands
- **Silk Farm Wildlife Sanctuary**, Concord—headquarters of New Hampshire Audubon Society
- **Amoskeag Mill Yard**, Manchester
- **Mt. Washington Observatory Resource Center**, North Conway

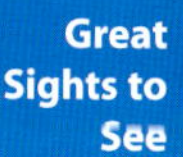

- **Abenaki Encampment and Shop**, Intervale
- **Twin Mountain Fish and Wildlife Center**—local wildlife and a water habitat exhibit called "Water on the Move"
- **Hampton Beach**—wide, sandy beach and a colorful boardwalk

Museums

New Hampshire Historical Society Museum, Concord
Museum of New Hampshire History, Concord
Manchester Historic Association Museum
Morse Museum, Warren
New Hampshire Farm Museum, Milton
Sandwich Historical Society Museum
Mount Kearsarge Indian Museum, Warner
Old Man of the Mountain Museum, Franconia Notch
Port of Portsmouth Maritime Museum
American Independence Museum, Exeter
Sandown Depot Railroad Museum
Nashua Historical Society
New Hampshire Antiquarian Society, Hopkinton
Peterborough Historical Society Museum
Museum of Childhood, Wakefield
Clark House Museum Complex, Wolfeboro
Cog Railway Museum, Mount Washington
Annalee Doll Museum, Meredith
New England Ski Museum, Franconia Notch

Lest We Forget

MONUMENTS

The **Cathedral of the Pines** in Rindge is an outdoor shrine and memorial. The Altar of the Nation recognizes all Americans who lost their lives in wars. The stone Memorial Bell Tower stands at the entrance to the pine grove. Four bronze sculptures designed by Norman Rockwell honor American women killed in battle.

In Francestown, a memorial stands to honor **Levi Woodbury** who served his state as legislator, judge, governor, and U.S. senator. He served his nation as treasury and naval secretary, and as Supreme Court justice.

The **Parson Main Monument** in Rochester honors the city's beloved Reverend Amos Main, parson from 1731 to 1774. Parson Main was loved by colonists and Native Americans.

The Arts

Currier Gallery of Art, Manchester
Manchester Institute of Arts and Sciences
New Hampshire Art Association, Manchester
Dartmouth College's Hood Museum of Art, Hanover
Arts and Science Center, Nashua
University Art Galleries, University of New Hampshire in Durham
Lamont Gallery, Phillips Exeter Academy in Exeter
League of New Hampshire Craftsmen, Concord
North Country Chamber Players, Sugar Hill
Archive Center of the Historical Society of Cheshire County, Keene
Peterborough Players Theater Company
New Hampshire Symphony, Manchester
New Hampshire Opera League, Manchester
Monadnock Music Concerts—summer concerts in several southwestern towns
Prescott Park, Portsmouth—summer-long arts festival with concerts, plays, films, and dance

To be, or not to be involved in the arts–that is the question. What is your answer?

Resorts and Inns

New Hampshire is known for its quaint towns and villages, picturesque countryside, cozy inns, and beautiful resorts.

Country Inns of the White Mountains
The Inn at Crotched Mountain, Francestown
The Manor on Golden Pond, Holderness
The Inn at Strawbery Banke, Portsmouth
The Governor Jeremiah Smith House Inn, Exeter
Three Chimneys Inn, Durham
The Inn at Maplewood Farm, Hillsborough
Tory Pines Resort, Francestown
Bedford Village Inn
The Meeting House Inn, Henniker
Staffords in the Field, Chocorua
Thistle and Shamrock Inn, Bradford
Potter Place Inn, Andover
The Hanover Inn
Shaker Inn at the Great Stone Dwelling, Enfield

The Balsams is a historic resort in Dixville Notch. Every four years, the first presidential election returns are announced from this magnificent resort in the White Mountains.

Roads and Trails!

Roads

Mount Washington Auto Road, Pinkham Notch, White Mountains

Kancamagus National Scenic Byway, White Mountains, follows the route of Chief Kancamagus and the Pennacook to Canada

Trails

The Appalachian Trail, crosses the White Mountains as it winds its way from Georgia to Maine

The New Hampshire Heritage Trail, 230-mile (370-kilometer) route from Massachusetts to Canada

The Welch-Dickey Mountain Trail, Eastern White Mountains

Portsmouth Harbor Trail, Portsmouth

Ellie's Woodland Walk at Ryefield Marsh

Wolfeboro Conservation Commission

Rail 'n' River Forest Trail, Eastern White Mountains

Great Glen Trails, Eastern White Mountains

New Hampshire has hundreds of miles of cross-country skiing trails.

Covered Bridges

New Hampshire has more than 50 covered bridges, most of them built in the 1800s. They have a roadway, wooden sides, and a roof. The wooden sides helped control a skittish horse. The bridges are numbered and the numbers appear on state maps.

Warner-Dalton Bridge, Warner village—built about 1800, is the oldest covered bridge in the U.S.
Winchester-Ashuelot Bridge, Ashuelot—crosses Ashuelot River
Swanzey-Slate Bridge, Westport—crosses Ashuelot River
Henniker-New England Bridge, Henniker—crosses Contoocook River
Cold River Bridge, North Sandwich
Keniston Bridge, Andover village—crosses Blackwater River
Albany Bridge, Conway

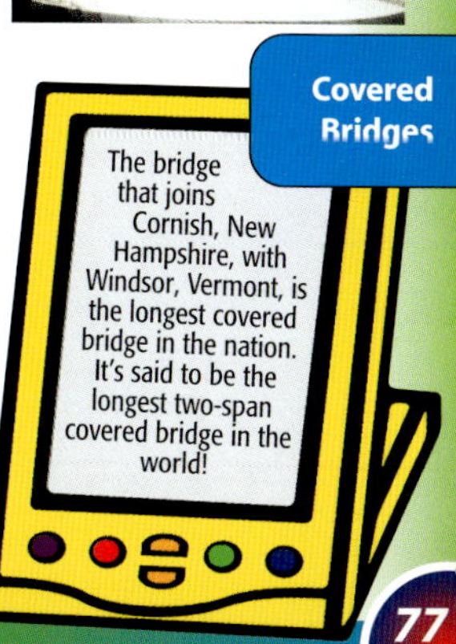

New Hampshire's Animals Include:

Skunk
Porcupine
Muskrat
Fox
Beaver

Moose
Bat
Raccoon
Chipmunk
Hare

Rabbit
White-tailed deer
Black bear
Coyote
Bobcat
Gray squirrel

Gray squirrels bury acorns. When they're out looking for the acorns they've buried, they usually find and dig up acorns other squirrels have hidden. Squirrels find acorns by smell, not by memory—they may find about 85 percent of buried nuts.

Some endangered and threatened New Hampshire animals:

Endangered:

Karner blue butterfly
Canada lynx
Small-footed bat
Bald eagle
Golden eagle
Peregrine falcon
Upland sandpiper
Roseate tern
Sunapee trout
Timber rattlesnake
Marbled salamander

Threatened:

Pine pinion moth
Marten
Common loon
Arctic tern
Common nighthawk
Eastern hognose snake

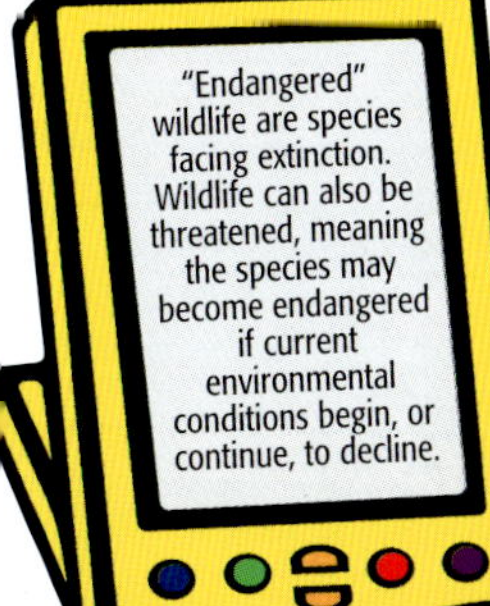

Birds
You may spy these birds in New Hampshire:
Purple finch
Chickadee
Nuthatch
Woodpecker
Hawk
Sparrow
Cardinal
Pine siskin
Brown creeper
Warbler
Kingbird
Phoebe
Meadowlark
Whippoorwill
Flycatcher
Loon
Hummingbird
Snow bunting
A hummingbird's wings beat 75 times a second–so fast that you only see a blur! They make short squeaky sounds, but do not sing.
Birds
80

Don't let these New Hampshire bugs bug you!

Dragonfly
Grasshopper
Katydid
Cricket
Praying mantis
Spittlebug
Ant
Ladybug beetle
Whirligig beetle
Tiger swallowtail butterfly
Firefly
Karner blue butterfly
Moth
Mosquito
Honeybee
Bumblebee

Bumblebee

Ants

Cricket

Praying mantis

Mosquito

Ladybug beetle

Grasshopper

Do we know any of these bugs?

Maybe... Hey, that ladybug is cute!

Whirligig beetles have two pairs of eyes—one pair looks above the water, the other under it!

Swimming in New Hampshire's waters:

Brook trout

Rainbow trout

Brown trout

Lake trout

Landlocked salmon

Black bass

Largemouth bass

Smallmouth bass

Pickerel

Yellow perch

White perch

Sea Critters

In New Hampshire's sea, you may see:

- Seal
- Dolphin
- Whale
- Shark
- Skate
- Ray
- Barracuda
- Eel
- Tuna
- Porpoise
- Turtle

Seashells

She sells seashells by the New Hampshire seashore!

Periwinkle
Slipper shell
Moon shell
Wentletrap
Whelk
Vampire shell
Bubble shell

Mussel
Oyster
Scallop
Shipworm
Cockle
Coquina
Angel wing

Sailors have used some types of whelk eggs to wash their hands. The whelk "egg soap" was called sea wash balls.

Vampire snails feed on the blood of their prey, usually without killing them. *Yuk!*

TREEMENDOUS!

THESE TREES TOWER OVER NEW HAMPSHIRE:

Spruce
Fir
Cedar
Hemlock
White pine
Maple
Oak
White birch
Tamarack
Ash
Basswood
Beech
Elm
Hickory

Wildflowers

Violet
Black-eyed susan
Daisy
Fireweed
Goldenrod
Butter-and-eggs
Purple trillium
Wild aster
Wild geranium
Jack-in-the-pulpit
Columbine
Jacob's ladder
Pink lady's slipper
Wood anemone
Buttercup
Queen Anne's lace

Cream of the Crops

Agricultural products from New Hampshire:

CHRISTMAS TREES

HAY

POTATOES

BEEF CATTLE

CORN

POULTRY

EGGS

APPLES

HOGS

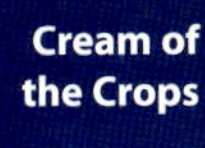

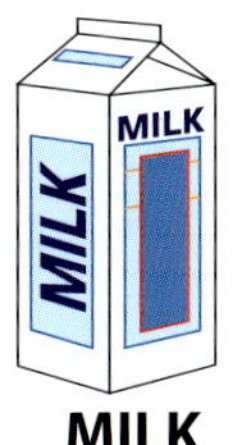

MILK

MAPLE SYRUP

The top of Mount Washington is said to be the **windiest place on earth!** Wind speed was recorded on April 12, 1934, at 231 miles (372 kilometers) per hour—that's three times as fast as most hurricanes! *Whoosh!*

New Hampshire is home of the Concord stagecoach. The country's **first regular stagecoach** runs went between Portsmouth and Boston.

New Hampshire became the first of the 13 colonies to declare its **independence from Great Britain** on January 5, 1776.

In 1719, the **first potato in the U.S.** was planted at Londonderry Common Field.

In 1787, Levi Hutchins of Concord invented the **first alarm clock**.

Built in 1938 at Franconia Notch, the Cannon Aerial Tramway is the **first aerial passenger tramway** in North America.

In 1899, Feelan O. Stanley (of Stanley Steamer fame) made the **first motorized ascent** of the Mount Washington auto road.

Every four years, New Hampshire holds the **first presidential primary**.

Festivals and Events

Celebrate!!!

Jazz Weekend and Festival, Portsmouth

Strawbery Banke Candlelight Stroll, Portsmouth

High Hopes Hot Air Balloon Festival, Milford

Spring Farming Day, Hollis

Festival of Fireworks, Jaffrey

Pumpkin Festival, Keene

Monadnock Music Craft Fair, Peterborough

League of New Hampshire Craftsmen's Fair, Sunapee

Dartmouth Winter Carnival, Hanover

Fall Foliage Festival, Warner

Meredith Chowder Festival

Attitash Equine Festival, Bartlett

Polar Express, North Conway

Frostbite Follies, Franconia

Music in the White Mountains Summer Festival, Lincoln and Sugar Hill

Quilt Festival, Sugar Hill and Franconia

July Fourth Festival, Littleton

Old Time Fiddlers' Contest, Stark

North Country Moose Festival, Pittsburg

Logging Competition and Fall Festival, Berlin

Holidays

Calendar

Martin Luther King, Jr. Day, *3rd Monday in January*	Groundhog Day, *February 2*	Presidents' Day, *3rd Monday in February*
Memorial Day, *last Monday in May*	Independence Day, *July 4*	Labor Day, *1st Monday in September*
Columbus Day, *2nd Monday in October*	Veterans Day, *November 11*	Thanksgiving, *4th Thursday in November*

Christmas, December 25

Sarah Josepha Hale was an author, editor, and educator from Newport. She worked to establish Thanksgiving as a national holiday.

New Hampshire is famous for...

the following foods!

Apples
Strawberries
Blueberries
Raspberries
Honey
Pumpkin Pie
Seafood Chowder
Pickles
Grilled Shrimp
Gingerbread
Smoked Salmon
Steamed Lobster
Pancakes and Maple Syrup
Red, White, and Blueberry Ice Cream

New Hampshire Works!

New Hampshire has a diverse economy with several major industries including the manufacturing of computers and software, machinery, military equipment, and plastic and leather products. Lumber and mining are also important industries.

Most New Hampshirites hold service-related jobs such as doctor, lawyer, teacher, politician, banker, and salesclerk. Government workers at the weather research center on top of Mount Washington compile weather information for the National Weather Service, the U.S. Army, and engineers around the country.

Only about 2 percent of New Hampshirites have jobs in agriculture. Farmers raise crops, dairy cows, beef cattle, hogs, and poultry. New Hampshire farmers grow more hay than any other crop. They use hay to feed cattle.

State Books & Websites

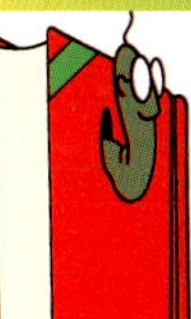

My First Book About New Hampshire by Carole Marsh
America the Beautiful: New Hampshire by Sylvia McNair
Kids Learn America by Patricia Gordon and Reed C. Snow
From Sea to Shining Sea: New Hampshire by Dennis Brindell Fradin
Hello U.S.A.: New Hampshire by Dottie Brown
Let's Discover the States: New Hampshire by the Aylesworths
The New Hampshire Experience Series by Carole Marsh

COOL NEW HAMPSHIRE WEBSITES

http://www.state.nh.us

http://www.newhampshireexperience.com

http://www.50states.com

http://www.netstate.com

New Hampshire Glossary

Glossary Words

amendment: change in, or addition to a bill, law, or constitution
colony: group of people who settle in a distant land, still under rule of country from which they came
constitution: document outlining the role of a government
endangered: in danger of becoming extinct or no longer living
historic: famous or important to the events of history
immigrant: person who comes to a new country to live
monadnock: isolated mountain that has resisted the process of erosion
notch: narrow pass between hills or mountains
overt: open, public, not hidden
primary: election for choosing candidates who will run in the final election
revolution: overthrow of a government with another taking its place
secede: voluntarily give up being a part of an organized group

New Hampshire Spelling Bee

Here are some special New Hampshire-related words to learn! To take the Spelling Bee, have someone call out the words and you spell them aloud or write them on a piece of paper.

Spelling Words

American Revolution	Mount Washington
apples	New Hampshire
brook trout	picturesque
colony	Portsmouth
Concord	purple finch
covered bridges	red spotted newt
Fort Constitution	Shakers
granite	skiing
inns	snow
ladybug	tourism

ABOUT THE AUTHOR...

CAROLE MARSH has been writing about New Hampshire for more than 20 years. She is the author of the popular *New Hampshire State Stuff Series* for young readers and creator along with her son, Michael Marsh, of *New Hampshire Facts and Factivities,* a CD-ROM widely used in New Hampshire schools. The author of more than 100 New Hampshire books and other supplementary educational materials on the state, Marsh is currently working on a new collection of New Hampshire materials for young people. Marsh correlates her New Hampshire materials to the New Hampshire learning standards. Many of her books and other materials have been inspired by or requested by New Hampshire teachers and librarians.

EDITORIAL ASSISTANT:

Billie Walburn

GRAPHIC DESIGNERS:

Al Fortunatti & Kathy Zimmer